CONVERSATIONS I'VE NEVER HAD

Caitlin Maling is from Western Australia. She has published poetry and nonfiction in *Best Australian Poems*, *Australian Poetry*, *cordite*, *Westerly*, *The Australian*, *Green Mountains Review*, *The Threepenny Review* and *Going Down Swinging* among others. She holds an MFA in poetry from the University of Houston, an MPhil in Criminological Research from Cambridge University and is a previous recipient of the John Marsden Poetry Prize. This is her first collection.

CONVERSATIONS I'VE NEVER HAD

CAITLIN MALING

FREMANTLE PRESS

For Colin

CONTENTS

I

The path to the dam

Our dads laid the lime-
stones. We couldn't lift
or nudge them with our toes
because of what we might catch
under. Like you can't put your feet
down the bottom, we were
too soft for yabbies and you
never dive from the bank
because the logs move
overnight. We kept to the surface,
struck with water-boatmen –
sun-skitterish pinpricks of life –
scattering away from the ripples
our fingers made. The year
they laid the path, my father
lived elsewhere and I
put my head under
for the first time,
past the warm spot,
swam deep,
it was so dark
and so cold,
there was no
way up.

To Robert Thompson

When you and I were ten you killed the baby.
I learnt about it on the radio
on the way to a Power Rangers birthday party.
That night, I drank Coke with the sugar left in
and we girls ran little pink circles
around each other for hours, only coming together
to cut to pieces someone's older brother.

Walking my little sister to school
the day after seeing you on the television,
I practised hardening my hands, tried picturing
her fingers as prison bars I had to break. For years
we would walk past a half-demolished home
the yard littered with stones like frags.
And for many days trying to feel the weight
of that brick in my hand
I developed imaginary callouses.

Now you and I have grown up together,
but I'm still not at that point
where I can take your mind in mine,
feel that little hand you felt pulling away
and only tighten my grip in response.

Sundays

waiting
for my father
to be late home
from surfing
my mother
would cut the sky
to ribbons
she would take
her sewing outside
and lay it on
the glass table
and with the kitchen scissors
tear silver
through the fabric
I would lie
under the table
and with
each precise injury
the cloth
bled sunlight
all over me
she was always
one of the
wise women
from the end of the world
picking apart
all she
created
she would never
turn her head

to see
if he had
come through the door

Donnelly River, 13

On the diving board above the dank dam water
Luke's lifting up my bikini top again.
A Ceauşescu baby, he arrived fully formed,
since then he's never not been touching one of us
and I think his parents named him after a Disciple
so he would always be surrounded by hovering ghosts and histories.
On the banks below, all my parents' friends are on 2nd marriages,
3rd homes, and my divorced parents who are 4th and 5th generation
go back just as far as this country lets us.

I wish the water wasn't water.

I'm sick of falling and righting and warming and cooling.
On the edge of the board, fighting off Luke's need for closeness,
I'm just jumping and jumping and hoping for wooden splintering or
     flight.
I try to name the things I see in time with jumping
and it's all paperbark-gum, snowy-gum, white-gum, red-gum, mallee.
Every family holiday in Australia might as well just be gum-gum-
gum-gum-gum-gum-gum. It doesn't matter that they have leaves
and sometimes flower, nothing falls,
the sky is always a eucalypt haze stretching,
making you think there's a horizon.

In the water, my sister has figured out how to lock her legs round my
     middle,
hands round my neck and push me under.
No matter how I land she's on me.
Each time she circles her arms and expects me to float,
I dive to where the water's only brown, like you're inside amber.

Only I know to follow the air up
once it erupts past your teeth like a hatred
and fights the sediment to the surface.
If I jump high and straight enough,
slash into the water, toes and fingers flexed down,
maybe I can plant myself among the weeds
and let the bottom-dwellers refine me, skin-fleck by skin-fleck.

Still things can change.
Dad was shovelling sand to protect his new baby
while I watched from the porch hammock,
my copy of Mishima on my chest like a confession stone.
The sound of the shovel in the half-granite dirt making me look
    over my pages
as a snake with storm-cloud skin came through the house,
down the steps, and straight at Dad still shovelling.
I said nothing
yet Dad turned in time, struck the head clean off.
The park owner said it must've been the mother-snake;
now the babies would die without her to dig them out.
Dad's wife made us move cabins anyways.

Now, next to my towel, the boy from the next door cabin is calling
    out,
asking me when I'm coming down
and if I want to walk back along the track together.
He's a high-jumper at WAIS, which means he's hot,
a boy who would normally throw stuff at me on the bus,
but here I'm the only teenage girl,
so he's willing to pretend for both of us that I'm hot too.

Last night I practised mothering his younger brother.
I held him on my lap, stroked his hair
and let the high-jumper see how I could care.
I told the boy his autism was ok with me.
But he'd never been told he was different
and he leapt from the top bunk like he was being axed from himself.
He ran round the small cabin punching the walls,
screaming *I'm not special, I'm not.*
His parents said I should leave,
so the high-jumper and I lay on the dirt between cabins,
closing our eyes, lightly pressing on their soft sweating folds,
pretending to see the stars.
When I opened mine he was leaning over me,
his head engulfed by the corona on my retina,
his face moving in a way stars shouldn't,
closer and closer,
and I didn't want any of that or in that way,
so I hit him with Mishima on the brow
and ran back to my cabin
to keep my stars on the roof above my bed.

I can see all the roads away from the campground from up here.
In the distance above the damn gums
is the jetstream of a plane
taking off or landing.

fourteen

we used to sit in the town square and dream drowning dreams
where life would swallow us whole and like jonah we'd be
transported fighting to somewhere foreign it was just you and me
at dusk and our laughter lingered like smoke and snaked its way
through the abandoned core of fremantle we'd journey
to the edges to beg for alcohol like children someplace foreign
do for food and when we got it take it back to our lair which lay
beneath the jungle gym where night would catch us alone and unawares
and the light of the bong was all that froze out our childhood fears
of the dark sometimes the homeless and hopeless would join us
on our journey and one a noongar took cigarettes from us
and in friendship offered a sniff and you who always dreamed deeper
than i took it and your eyes filled with the same silver as the paint
and you went up and away from me while i plagued by vertigo
watched you get higher and tried to tether the remains of you to me
so that come 1130 when your mother picked us up from where
we were meant to be at least half of you was there to greet her

Asphodel

When I think *we girls,*
I think *Summer of the Seventeenth Doll*. Our summer,
when we caught the train back from playing pool
with the US sailors in Port
and I fell asleep on your lap
the sailor hat I'd earned wedged on.

Back home, you have that hat with all our treasures lined up,
like the kewpie dolls Roo would bring Olive
back from the canefields.

I remember being in Innisfail after Larry,
the thicket of palm leaves and sugar cane capturing the road
and on the TV that night a man crying, dead bananas at his feet:
me dad started this farm and now me sons won't be able to work it.

And I wish someone had taught me
to hide photographs in bottom drawers,
a lock of hair under my pillow. The three of us
kept ours in different colours – red, blonde and black –
us pretty girls all in a row.

Where I live now, bananas cost 70 cents a pound.
I have no way to explain how precious they are.

sixteen

in our magical years our
bad haircuts black lipstick years
we laughed the night to pieces
threaded youth through the streets
trailing smoke losing hours
we knew we were starblessed
using our cigarettes
to stitch our names
in the gaps between
cassiopeia and orion
we were selkies we
were sirens we were
the itch at the top
of a man's mouth he
tries to ignore
circes we drifted
our island down the tce
collecting pigs

Shark days

Dad hands me the knife as I tie two one-kilo weights to my waist like penances. He says *it's rough today, onshore, current'll take you out*; he says *I remember when you were young, you'd run at the ocean arms open. It's cold*, I say, *visibility's way down*. But I take the knife, strap it to my ankle over the neoprene, thread my flippers through my belt, and set out round the rocks for the edge.

At a break in sets we jump, swim straight at the horizon – the one they tugged the whale to last summer. It had beached and the town came to pour water, anoint it, until the smell set in and the boat was sent for.

Dad pushes past in a froth and pauses over a patch of reef 30 feet down. *I can free dive 60,* he says, *you should be able to manage 40.* Dad points at the abalone growing, points at the knife, hands me a net and heads down for a cave I can't quite make out.

I dive, just grab hold of the reef and let the current shake me. I can't pull the knife without letting go and I can't let go without surfacing, so I wait for Dad up top, facing my mask down so I don't see how far offshore we are. He rises, trailing his spear and the blood of a pink snapper shedding scales.

When they towed the whale out the sharks came in. The sea was a fisherman's moon, red and billowing, gone in the morning.

Dad sends me back down, until I break the knife trying to split the abalone from the reef and we take the long way back to the bay, though it's dusk and October is the end of shark migration.

Bloodlust

there is a bloodlust
to ordinary time
tick of clock or heart
that pulse
your neck and jawbone hide
how deep in the retina
thoughts dance out
to earthquakes on the tv
the breath hissing
like a pot on the boil
(thank god it wasn't here)
at each stop sign
each school crossing
the quickening of ligaments
over accelerator
the sinuous impulse
just to push

eighteen

After the man
hit the toilet door
with the cricket bat
(his girlfriend was inside),

because we had been smoking
since 9 pm and now the sun
was fracking all the anger
(suzie was mad her nails

were dirty and mags
no one had complimented
the cactus and I that everything
was turning yellow)

out of us and into the room
with all the other smoke,
I got in my car
(it was yellow),

to go home, or to work
and at the top of banksia hill
cut the power, "went stealth"
let the car roll itself.

Over the river,
a thousand kites rose
and all the way down the hill
I didn't see any tangle

or fall. They ate the sky
and were so beautiful,
green and red teeth,
so beautiful I didn't know.

Concessional: Cassandra to Helen

I admit
I always wanted,
I always wanted more.
I always wanted oceans,
men on oceans,
a shore of men,
teeming, little bows,
little arrows, firing up
from the shore at me
who was always wanted.

When I said I didn't,
didn't want, I meant
didn't want in the sense that
I didn't want this
not to come to pass,
to the extent that I tried
not to want, but
I always wanted.

Helen you were one
of them. They fired
you answered: you fired
and you were answered. Helen
you were always the shore
men so sought
and you sought to be
that shore so
fired upon. Helen you
have no walls.

I let you –
The temple is beautiful.
I let you –
The moon is adrift.
I left you –
Quiet the.
I let you –
Fall in stones.
I let you –
Bring the roof to pieces
of light.

Pine

i
And everyone knows how it ends.
With the body pine-sweet
and rotting in the plantation past Wellup,

from where, unwitting, we would bring needles
to our mantles those chainsaw Christmases,
when we took the ute out the highway
and I learnt to lean down on the blade
'cause it takes all my weight to cut,

my stepfather saying *they aren't natives*
anyways, they are only there to be taken down,
you can't thieve something that shouldn't been
in the first place.

ii
Driving round the Donnelly we crest
among the jarrah to a massacre
of old-growth, pine saplings creeping
with a tender hunger,

air sugar-thick as blood or toffee and silent,

until Mum says it was Mario the sometimes magician
who dabbled in children's parties
that done it. He felt wrong and they'd walked out on him
at the Conti that night, his fingers curling round
a blonde. *His Eyes.* Mum says. *His Eyes. Didn't belong*

anywhere. But everyone knows a white man
who drives a white car and likes to stand too close.

iii
Nights, I find myself walking down Bayview.

Above the Council Chambers,
those same Norfolks gesture
like they must've to the others.

I climbed one once as a child,
wrapped my legs round the trunk
and let the bark bleed my palms
just to keep myself from leaping.

Now, my stilettoes stabbed into the dirt
are all the roots I have.

I would be easy to fell
(if a car stopped) I'd go sweetly.

After a girl goes missing

The pots are still dropped and pulled at 4am,
but no-one fishes near seal rock for weeks, out where the shadows
of sharks and seals are interchangeable.

Her next door neighbour stops taking his tractor to collect
bogged tourists.
Down at the café, his wife tells her sister his back just wasn't up to it,
but he tells his wife how in dreams he sees himself driving over
    something half-hidden
and the tractor is left on the curb to rust.

For six months someone has seen her someplace else on the Highway,
from Geraldton to Jurien to Green Head to Cataby to Lancelin to
Yanchep to Wanneroo to Perth.

Nearby, on the New Road, the sand dunes move closer
and recede again.

The Blokes drive around the roads with their roo-guns in back
and the   *You Are Now Leaving*............
has to be replaced four times,
the spent bullets clumping together with the emu droppings.

Walking back from the Scout Hall towards the ocean,
it is possible to mistake the corrugated iron horse with his wise man
for both a saviour and a thief.

In the newly released parcel of land out by the windfarm,
the President of Dandaragan Shire names a suburb after her.

This is progress.

Out-of-towners, city-folk, sea-changers move in, smooth the hills and build
variations of the same seaside, each with a different painting
of sand above an overgrown cottage-rose couch.

And by the time her parents are buried,
that summer is remembered as the one
when *fisheries screwed us on the catch*,
when the skippers instructed the deckies to *throw back*,
when the ocean floor crawled with whites
and five-legged kings *even a child could catch*.

Lust

We shared too much of each other
that night
        beyond the railings
                at the Roundhouse,
clutching ground
which   broke
and   crumbled
at our touch.

How the dark
sucked at the couple
on the sand below,
who bobbed
   about like buoys
   and bound their bodies together.

I still see you,
standing above me
against the stars
        which hung about
                like flies
and pestered with radiance.

The moon looking on
as you lowered your head
to feed.

Things we learn from our Father

Age 7
Not to turn our backs on the ocean early,
To walk backwards out of surf
One eye on the horizon,
The other on the white water
Breaking from the right.

We are taught when to jump,
When to dive, how to roll
In a ball and how to
Grab the reef with both hands
And not to notice the cuts after.

We know when to talk behind the break,
How the surf is timeless
In the sense that
When we are waiting, watching
For you to paddle back in,
The distance is measured in waves not hours.

Age 10
We know to throw our towels in front of us
On the black sand of Yallingup
Over and again
To get back to the toilets above.

And when the rain starts to fall over Smiths
We know the one tree
And the one way
To place them over the limbs,
To huddle together

Only slightly damp,
While the surfers cut across our sightline –
An armada against the elements –

And when you prowl your way to the shore,
We know not to mention the cold.

Age 13
From the front seat
Of your Holden
We learn the pull of the moon,
How to spot the tides
And sets from clifftops,

While the radio speaks
In the language of the winds,
So we slowly learn
To narrate oceans
But to never utter a sound
When the hourly forecast is announced.

Age 16
We are taught to drive the back roads,
Scything through the gravel,
Pursuing the next
Break
At breakneck paces.

We know not to trust speed limits
But to trust that
Round the most unlikely corners

The ocean will appear,
Waves feral in this wilderness,

But by now we know better
Than to speak of fear.

Age 19
We learn to leave you behind,
To make our way
Slightly slower
From beach to beach,
Hours undefined
By weather forecasts.

We know to bring the sand
To your bedside,
Where it sits
Tapped of all its ferocity.

And we learn how the sea
Welcomes its own.
How it doesn't roar
But circles.

And we know now
How to paddle back alone
And to walk away,
One eye on the horizon,
The other where you lie

In the white water
Breaking from the right.

II

Things I missed about Cervantes while in Cambridge

I wound the streets with a man I hardly knew
as he told me stories of heads under fields,
golden clocks and buildings with insides on outsides,
I wanted to shout, to tell him it is so beautiful here
it drives my mind to suspicions
about who placed those trees there just so
and curved the river round so singularly,

that here I'm lost within the wealth of history,
tarnished brass so plain it's ugly, and that for all
the years people have built here and all
the tales embedded in each brick,
I miss nothing more than the simple honesty of the ocean,
the openness of the sea.

Holiday

Perth from above is a cockroach.
It sits there, brown and laconic, and
the microwave of summer can't shift it,
suburbs, like legs, twitching intermittently.
You fly in over rivers
dried and stretched like junkies' veins,
wells and damns punched around them.

Suddenly, on the ground below you,
all you see is water, the populace
congealed at the edges of the Swan,
scuttling among the sand.

Back in Perth

There is a bone-sadness here as
I speak with my sister in the hollowed air
of what is raw between us.
Our hands take flight at one another
the unsaid flaring over coffee.
The blood we share is sluggish
clogging the afternoon sticking
our words to our sinuses.
I wish I had not flown 20 hours over
15 countries in darkness only to meet you
and the parts of the self I left behind.

Medea to Jason

i will cut
        the stillness from you
the silence
        from your throat
thrust forceps in your ears
        and cram
all you never spoke
        past your optic nerve
you thought you could
fashion your tongue
into a chastity belt
        hold me virginal
        behind clenched teeth
                when you part your lips
                to her

i will move
        so swiftly
                that you will wish
                        you had already
                                scattered my ashes

                        you cannot keep
                        me in the quiet
                        your brain
                        is my honeycomb
                        you were wrong
                        to think
i wouldn't suck you dry

For my Lady M

When Judith dashed the head from Holofernes
it was you that spurted out.

Without you there could never have been
Real-Housewives-of-Any-City.
Whenever one of those witches tosses
her hair & withholds sex
you are there, stage left.

You showed me how to plot
against infants.
You knew, that although I was 11 & my brother 1
he & I both had our forces,
our positions to cement.

You watched over me
as I lynched his Teletubby above the stairs
leaving it swaying from my school stocking
as I descended.

That night I dreamt of Tinky Winky
& his purple handbag
marshalling fields of overlarge lops
against me.

When my sister started dating a Duncan
I was immediately suspicious.
I have yet to dispatch him
but I'm trying.

Now speaking to Mark about my graduate workshop
about allegiances, alliances & strategies,
I ask "What would Lady M do?"
& he's all "You know she dies right."
& I'm like "Bitch, please."

& I tell him how in reality
you got divorced,
took half the kingdom,
logged all those stupid trees
& caught a boat to Spain
where you had a string of lovers
& ate shellfish with your fingers,
letting their flesh gather at your cuticles.

Truth be:

You invented what we mean when we say
"man the fuck up".
No way you would've killed yourself
over unwashed hands.

Lament for Cervantes

Cervantes sits
a big dirt mouth
a jutting smile to the North.
On the towns one incline
slumbers the club,
where on plastic-draped tables,
beer-battered fish perspires.
Five men,
each of them called Tommo,
sit firing-squad straight along the bar
and the air is drowning with the new road,
when it's not it's
THE CATCH and
THE SEASON.
50 metres to the left,
over the parched bowls green
then the pockmarked oval,
(CERVANTES vs JURIEN Saturday)
is The Tav where
the deckies –
a flock of Chookas and Simmos –
perform a slow losing dance
to the TAB.
On Saturdays,
a backpacker hired with his guitar
plays U2 covers only just heard
over the throes of the trots
being thrashed out to the North,
a mixture of sweat and sea in the air.
There are gaps at the bar.
My hand can just reach and receive

and in passing conversations
is the dying language
of Kings and Whites.
Outside through the town
for-sale signs glisten
like sharpened teeth
and in the night,
circling,
gulls cry
and are lost to the moon.

The fish

The roller-door rattles/raises and my stepfather brings in a fish,
flops it on the counter in front of my mother so hard its eyes
continue to jiggle for just a moment. *It's a dhuey* he says voice rising/
falling like a buoy. My mother takes pains to examine it closely
running her fingers against the grain of the scales before calling
Girls come and see what Greg has brought us
in her smoker's rasp. My sister and I rise from our cards to stand
around/above the fish, our now eight eyes watching its now still eye
singular. Hannah plays up being grossed, gagging, flailing/faux-fainting,
I counter with a mimicry of hunger all salivation and watering eyes.
Over our mincing/moaning we come to agree one thing that
My this is a big fish, a pronouncement which makes Greg
throw his arms around the two of us and squeeze, leaving us
smelling the sea/salt on him. *I look after my girls* he says and
on this there can be no disagreement for just as there was a fish today
there will be one tomorrow and there was one yesterday. If we were
to measure love in fish, my stepfather would be a fishmonger.

Marriage

My husband holds me to him like a clam shell,
arms clenched like barnacles
to the jetty at Point Walter.

It's 4 am and I can't sleep.
He has settled his weight around me
sandbags keeping out the tide.

His ribcage on my back opens and
closes with a surety that forces
my breath with his.

On our bedside table is
the tea he made me at 3 am, next to that
a wedding picture his eyes clear and unflinching.

When I fall asleep at 5 am I know
that if I stop breathing in my sleep,
he will be able to breathe for both of us.

Eurydice speaks

after Edward Hirsch

i
You didn't know how I hid my head in darkness,
a child in the oak avoiding moonlight.

How I could touch with only closed curtains,
snuffed candle lingering in hair, in breath.

How your skin burnt through my sleep
so I woke all mornings on the boil, a little more

evaporated, a little less, than the day before.

ii
My father hung light all over my mother
as though she was his hatstand. Across years

she was blinded to any other image;
my face was his and in her own
she saw only the places he had touched.

On our marriage when you took my chin in your hands
I knew I could never hate myself so much,
nor love you enough, to become your mirror,

to see myself only through your fingertips.

iii

When you played my name back into being
I remembered what it meant to want,

felt the drowning sound of longing
reborn at the back of my throat.

You peeled dark off me like autumn leaves
leaving me bare, blood already blistering

the thick of you on the tip of my tongue,
Orpheus. Orpheus the song of you

in my footsteps, almost enough
to dance me out of shadows.

Not quite enough to stop me
slipping your name from my lips,

the turn of your head, and the darkness.

Aftershock

for Christchurch

i
The skull of a nine-month-old
is no harder than a rockmelon,
with wobbly fissures
that can only balance
momentarily on the atlas.
And this is all there is
to cradle all that potential.

ii
An infant's casket
differs from an adult's
in that the wooden box
is heavier than what remains
of the body.
The weight of all that empty air
enough to suffocate
a church-full.

iii
Did you know
the word for children's teeth
is deciduous?
They are the leaves
of the mouth
that fall only at the beginning
of life's second season.

iv
After the earthquake
that small body,
in that white box,
had not had the time
to unfurl even one leaf.
And it's hard to believe
it took so much to
destroy so little a thing.

III

generation why

we're broken
you and I
not pleasantly imperfect
in a crooked nose way
broken
like a chipped front tooth
you have to grimace to hide
a greenstick fracture
of a relationship

our hell is a 3-legged race
at a work bonding function
limping
towards the finish
dragging
one foot
then the other
your leg
tied to mine in twine
still trying to beat each other
over the line

I can hear you screaming
over email
colon dash zero :-0
about your entitlement
to a quarter acre
diagnosing each other
over google
I lob paranoia at you
while you serve back

a portion of bipolar
you found on a forum

we were born
breaking
my ringtone is in my blood
you didn't know
what life was
before the internet
we stand at arms
bearing iPhones
somewhere along the way
there will be no more need for laughter
our jaws locked at one another
lol

Leonora 2010

lady at the store tells me i'll be fine
that those abos won't bother me because
they know what will happen if they do   &
they mainly stick amongst themselves anyway
the night is flawless above me   &
it's a 200 metre walk to the pub
punctuated only with the sound of a dog barking
some forgotten vengeance at the moon
at the pub I get directed to the side of the bar
where everybody looks like me   but
with haircuts and jeans from the 1990s
these people smile and greet me like i'm
something lost   they've just found under a cupboard   &
after dinner someone offers to walk me home for protection

somewhere nearby   behind bars   children sleep out their childhood
fathers stitch lips together   &
slowly unlearn the language of their past

Gendericide

There are many ways to kill the female child:
a small incision that does not tear
bricks, bullets, and other ballistics
coathangers and knitting needles
ropes, torn strips of cotton
the withdrawal of love, of food
a slender needle, a bubble of air
money, fear, hatred
a bucket of water
a car with the exhaust blocked
fists and the subtlety
of a pink envelope.

Easter up the Gascoyne

I cross downriver after the floods.
Upriver the Junction Hotel splays
all its hundred years around a gum,

like the innards of a kangaroo
ill-met with a road train. Once this was
the oldest pub in Western Australia,

where cameleers sandy from racing
saw Djinns in the red dirt wind. Since then,
the rest of the state has been in drought

so fierce it has cracked the riverbeds
to parchment. But here in this desert,
among waterlogged cattle carcasses

floating like forgotten languages,
the white ibis has returned and stands
with wings stark as a hieroglyph,

before casting into the new depths
to snatch forth an infant tiger snake
writhing. In the rear-view mirror

the babe draws out and slackens,
as the wings take flight
and I keep driving. I will be at

Burringurrah by morning. I will
climb the rock past the point of its naming
and from the apex, the land, larger

than any scripture, will be dotted
with the spilt ink of spent rains. Somewhere
something is greening.

TV pastoral

I should be a person with a catchphrase,
capable of shepherding inner-city youths
with bibles, basketballs, even origami,
while saying *do unto others* or *you can be anybody*.
I would like to be anybody who believes
what the television preaches, to *let's get excited
about your life*. My head gets so full. I could paint you,
but they play five episodes of *16 & Pregnant*
in a row. Love is so ordinary. I want for nothing,
unless I can have a signature fragrance,
a personal tan: burning bush or desert storm.
There's a moment when you turn the TV on,
when the screen slowly fades into a green,
it's a sunrise of sorts – you can hear birdsong in it.

At the Ballarat Art Gallery

we saw these hills before their clearing,
how the trees

wove the light into a feather coat,
each frame a different wing of the land,

never the tip, always in flight.
In the room next door Nolan's Leda

is indistinguishable from the swan,
they stretch away and towards each other;

a particular parting, a cleft.
Outside your house the remaining gums

pinprick the ridges and I watch
your shadow in mine till the sun parts us.

If I was to write the truth, it would be
that I wish I felt more at each of these partings

than I do.

The break

To prevent tragedy the brush must be cut at angles,
no less than ten metres between squares.

Here my ancestors planted the buffalo grass
where it burns too hot for the native plants to seed

and we need these squares between land
to stop it sparking all the ways to our homes.

After her third institutionalisation they suggested
that my aunt's cingulate cortex be severed,

there was too much leaping between lobes.
Now I am the oldest member of my father's family

not to have undergone inpatient treatment
for whatever fire caused my grandmother's suicide

and the beating my grandfather gave which sparked it.
I try to hold my line. To be the space

large enough to let it all burn out.
But out of my native climate I arc and arc.

Hector

When the snakes spit
                this truth into my mouth
                I held your name between my teeth   refused
                        to swallow

                        What use truth
                What of your body

Hector

all the sand

                the waves grooming you
                                for ocean burial

                                                Hector

Hector

                I tried

told the gulls
                so they might tell you

                                        Hector

my tongue makes landfall
                        against you

Hector

sure one
shore one

all the notes I wrote grew feathers
flight

Hector

where are we now

there's water in the sky
the oceans rising over the walls

the fire
the fire

yesterday or tomorrow

Hector

my tongue is rough with warnings

Hector

all I can do

is beat my heart at you

Living waters

When Gorgon was still unravelling
            from the underside
                        of our white-bellied dreaming
and mining first came to the Pilbara like a dog
            nosing for bones,
the underground creek system was destroyed
and no matter of praying
                        could make it lay down.

There thousands of Yulparija died of drought.
            The rest shuffled to Bidyadanga,
                        in the saltwater country of the Karajarri,
where Elders have started to paint the Jila,
            for grandchildren who will never know the desert
and its waters.

These paintings map ways of remembrance
            I can only ever trace the hollow of.
I will fly to Perth in the morning
            with my husband's desert-money
                        from minding metal silos that hold fuel
to push the ore-train screaming like the ghost of a serpent
            through the Pilbara.

Wherever I fly in this land I'm thirsty.

A380 letter

Flying away from all that commotion of home tongues.
The ocean solid as sheet glass,

physics says if I dropped
both the water and I would shatter.

But I have little interest in understanding
how to piece myself together.

In the water below are Irukandji jellyfish.
They fire stingers like invisible arrows

causing paralysis, palpitations
and a sense of impending doom.

In 1964 Barnes caught one and shot himself
just to prove their syndrome existed.

Sometimes in the same way
I look at photos of you.

IV

Writing to Perth from Houston

In places which are not home,
even the three-lettered 'car' is foreign.

As each new thing snatches the name of an old,
this thievery is just another little grief.

Finger at the pen, slowly creeping words
together like sand into isthmuses,

all each line can do is trace
your surf-bitten contours and every word

that breaks this paper shore
crossed your reef-bound one.

Moving is too close to mourning.

North of the river

When you jump off the cliffs you show me:
this is your side of the river, where the stone lies below.
You coax me off the rocks, *the water* you say, *lovely, love*.
Falling, I wonder who jumped here first,
set the knowledge of these stones down.
There's more uncertainty to the second jump, the third, fourth.
You start to make me leap first and when I'm dropping
I don't know if you will wait for me to land before leaping.

Still dripping on the carpet of your room you tell me:
that I am only as alive as the light bulb
and you make me stare at it until I can keep it when I close my eyes.
Electricity you say. You rub my hand across the carpet,
touch it to the bedframe, a small spark, *this is what you are,
not flame*. Out your window I see my side of the river
but I don't know it all from here, the browns and greens solid.
Can you only know the river when you're underneath it?

How we fall. How you come to mean it. Closer
to your cliffs. On the phone you ask me to come
or you would if I answered. I'm scared to look out my windows
200 metres inland, cupped to suburbia, you appear in light bulbs.
I won't go to the jetty. I won't go to where there's water.

Not the last time I saw you, but the last time I listened,
you said you had unfurled yourself
like the light, like the rocks don't bounce but grind
themselves from the rubble to the water. We sat outside,
you had marked where your stones would lay with razors.
In the hospital your room had no windows, no glass,
you were only allowed the sun, no light bulbs.

I want you to know the bayous running like ill-made filaments
through this city. Water is not trusted here, they girder it concretely
as if hardening the banks into scars will protect them.
I've never seen the bottom, never seen the black moccasins,
never met a person who has caught an alligator.
In hurricane season you wait for me on overpasses.
The pact we never made: not to jump alone.

Shark nights

2000, I get in a car with a stranger.
He cries silently across the river,
my friend who knows him, somewhat,
rides shotgun and acts like she doesn't notice.
The next school year when we're distant –
locker-mates but no longer bus-buddies –
she pulls me up to say *I can't believe you*
were so rude after what happened to his Dad.
It was one of those things the town remembers,
the family man taken from his sea kayak
50 metres offshore. The shark strikes, circles, leaves.
We've been seeing it every year since.

Now in my gulf coast home,
I hook family photos in semicircles to the walls,
open, like rows of jaws.

Hurricane season

Babies born into arctic dark –
24 hours of night – have minds
more easily widowed of sense.

Now Gulf, wrap your humidity around me,
your currents and flocks of migrants,
in your September. Beached, let pelicans

animate the sky, my lips to curve
and eyes to wonder, keep me,
my feet, whole in the mud of the flats.

Sky, dear yellowing, failing light,
fat with rain, blow the winds
that stop the egret mid fish-dance;

allow me one more season of sense,
of knowing the names for these:
stone-turner, curlew, plover, hawk and gull.

If you take one roof from the houses,
take them all. Open the suburbs up.
Make rockpools from the cul-de-sacs

where I cling mollusc-like
to possibility; to shore:
an idea of a horizon, where

after rain, in the eddy of brown waters
at knees, at waist, you rise,
you raise me up, remind me

that I was born to dry heat, drought,
on the grit-banks of a river widening
through limestone, seeking salt, seeking

sea, in September,
lightning strikes outback of the breakers;
the horizon appears in an instant.

Soon darkness.
Soon, light.

Town

Mum says there's a dip,
business is slow,
> stores are shutting earlier.
I leave and return with the markets,
> read the ASX for nostalgia.

Town's at the interchange of people and profit,
so I invest in the desert:
> the oil field under Coober Pedy
> that will feed our cars for decades.

One day I'll put my money where my home is.

I tell Mum I've almost enough to fly back,
buy myself a house in town
> walking distance to The Strip.
I've almost enough of myself,
> not to be swallowed in the cracks outside Gino's,
> > the Roundhouse's rough salt-wind.

Word of the town
refracts through the wires,
to where I eat sfogliatelle
and read small letters about our Dockers:
> how proud the town;
> how well they faced defeat.
Now we crumble into hope
> of the next year and the next,
forecast seasons, skies, the market's resurgence,
> a swell, a sea

breeze that comes in everyday at three,
the one my skin still goosepimples for
as I warm my lips with Americano
and progress's burnt-toast smell
blown in from Baytown.

I don't know how to name
all the things I'm missing.

Tacit knowledge

Driving back from Zavalla at 5 pm along some road towards Courpsville
wondering exactly what I'm meant to watch the ice do on the bridge.

This morning a snake came up from the undergrowth
and I didn't know whether it could kill me.

It wasn't the diamond-headed death-bringer of my childhood;
nor does the maxim of if it's long it's deadly hold up in Texas.

From the wrong side of the road
I rang Mum in her new house. She laughed at me,

then said they had a 2 metre dugite living in their shed.
She was worried I was driving at dusk

and told me to watch for roos and I didn't correct her.
But what I want to know (as I drive past a dead thing with horns) is:

why can't someone tell me if deer are crepuscular?

Homesick song

I miss you sea-shallow with blue-sky flotilla
of surf-spray above the armada of adolescents
at the pilon dive-bombing the sea-bottom
below the tea-rooms all sea-shell ear-rim mauve
in the long sea-depth darkness of the pines
and has there ever been a comfort more
than your sea-salt pine-sweet sea-air
where the coconut oiled sea-swept hair
of everyone you have ever known
makes the twilight as viscous as the sea
and you need your whole eye to see
to the end of the sea-pier past the pelican
on the shark-watch tower to where the sea
parts for the break with tenderness

Family rule

You can't be on the sand
unless you are willing to be in the ocean.
Wintering in Tasmania
near Devil's Sinkhole,
where Dad says he used to jump
the 100 metres to the water
and free-dive through the tunnels
to the open ocean,
I caught hypothermia,
sky pink with cold
as my limbs went heavy and still.

I'm sick now of recklessness and bravery.
I've found a warm bed,
enough money for 1000-count linens
and my pictures to hang on a wall
in this other country.
No more are the days
of Dad wearing his Viking helmet
around his caravan,
beating his chest, shouting
we have lungs meant to scream
bloody in battles or storm.

You don't need this, he'd say
collecting me at lunch from school,
what you need is the surf.
And he'd take me to the back break
when the winter dumpers rolled in,
leave me to find my way back up
from under the white-water.

Sometimes I miss the man I should've been
if I stayed under longer,
learnt the limits of my lungs.
In Houston now, the weed is storm-tangled
and I take puckered steps
among domestic debris,
into an ocean that doesn't rage,

but every time I still wade out,
put my head down as far as it will go,
tell it to *test me,*
come on, test me.

Terroir

For the Kevin John Chardonnay 2011

The wine arrives in Houston bubble-wrapped,
harvested the last summer I spent south among the grapes,
on sun-drenched dirt and eucalypt-dappled roads.
That December, under the blue moon,
the days and nights stayed over 30,
the land dried and off the beaches
seagrasses yellowed and lightened
to the brilliant straw of this wine.
My body is a calendar of such summers;
an accumulation of freckles and lines.
Like wine we carry our terrain with us.
My hand raising the glass, aged under the same skies
as the grapes it holds, but not as sweetly.
My tongue reacquaints with these grace notes
of citrus and vanilla under high heat
and I remember home can be a very simple thing,
a glass from a bottle received unbroken,
a mouth all it takes to be grateful.

You will wear white

when we were fourteen
we said we would never marry
we would wait out our old age together
and use men only for sex
because we weren't lesbians or anything like that
we would have an apartment
in any city but here
and earn enough money
so we no longer had to
trade kisses with US sailors on leave
for 50 mls of vodka
it would be you and me
and a closet filled with only black clothes
and we hadn't decided yet
if there would be pets
or overnight guests
but we knew there would never
be husbands or babies
or illness or ageing
and we would always know
how to speak to one another
and what we were doing together tomorrow
now you ring me
from your side of the country
to tell me
you're marrying your babydaddy
and you're wearing white

How I spent my 18th year

After I leave acting school (drop-out)
I take a job as operations manager at an electronics store
and start rehearsing how to be normal. I grow
my hair and nails out and learn the difference
between ash- and honey-blonde highlights. I fall for
the floor manager who is 15 years older than me
and once was a trainee for the NBL but he rebelled
to go to the beach one too many times. He said he
got a spiritual connection to the sand, man,
that he measured in wristbands from Bali
and his tan. He might go back to basketball
sometime, but his life philosophy is *take it one*
day at a time, like the surf, it comes and then it goes,
it flows, I flow, you know? So day after day
I print price stickers, relabel computers, I get
manicures with the cashiers and adopt
their wisdom *never get both gel tips and colours;*
only girls from the northern suburbs would wear
two different animal prints; 5 inch heels are sexy,
6 inches is slutty. When we go out for Friday drinks
with the kids from the Carrington store I drink
Jager Bombs until I'm ready to stand in a circle
and *come on Eileen, oh I swear (what he means)*
then it's midnight and I go back to the floor manager's
to sit and smoke and he plays Red Hot Chili Peppers
and *'Under the bridge' was written for me, when I listen*
it's like I'm listening to myself. When I wake up
there's permanent marker on my legs, an arrow
pointing *enter here*, and we laugh. No-one
ever asks why I left acting school, but if they did

I would tell them I never wanted to be on the stage
I only ever wanted the taste of other people's
words in my mouth. Something to chew.

Directions

Karijini by way of Cataby, Geraldton, Dongara, Carnarvon,
Exmouth; by way of the Brand; by way of driving out at
midnight, by way of fences and flame trees and bardies; by
way of moonlight and the Dog Star, the Cross and Corona
Australis; by way of 4 am, by way of bone silence, by way
of somnambulance amid truckies and road trains; by way
of midday in the banana fields; by way of midnight in
the campground; by way of hollowed and halved water
receptacles bearing wine, by way of pretensions, of West
Cape Howe, Leeuwin Estate, Pendleton; by way of air-
mattresses; by way of song of burrowing frogs; by way of
days at the beach, the sea, the ocean, the Indian, the blue,
the deep, the coral, the bungies, the reef, Ningaloo; by way
of the wobbygong, escaping by way of currents and belly-
up, by way of floating, by way of Turquoise Bay; by way
of salt-grit in your hair; by way of saturation, of summer
storm, by way of tents with broken ramparts; by way of
electricity, of lightning; by way of the dunes, the thunder
of sand, an inland tsunami; by way of your fingertips, cold
cracking metatarsals and calluses; by way of tyres, by way
of gravel roads, by way of rust in the undercarriage, rust in
the red-dirt, rust in the sunset; by way of fraternisation in
the long grass; by way of fish'n'chips in Dampier, by way
of the peninsula, the salt isthmus; by way of the boab; by
way of turning inland, turning inward; by way of distance,
the peaks of Mungaroona Range, the decay of Maroona
iron mine; by way of wild donkeys, lost camels, far-off
dingoes, gnarled goannas; by way of track; by way of Bee
Gorge, Kalamina Gorge, Yampire Gorge; formed by way of
dolomite and Mount McRae shale; built by way of granite,
by way of tessellations and the fractal of mineral sands;

only seen by way of the microscope, overlooked in the
rear-view mirror by way of your eyes, the iris, the retina;
by way of mistaking your tongue for the Milky Way; by
way of waking to red dust on skin, ochre touch-painted; by
way of hiking to Kermit's Pool the cool of water in desert;
by way of packing-up; by way of defenestrating apple
cores at 140 kmph; by way of racing utes to no destination;
by way of signs counting down 800 km to Perth, 700 km to
Perth, 600 km to Perth.

Acknowledgements

This collection is for my family: Colin, Hannah, Rowena, Greg, Charlie, Finn, Ray and Jill. Special thanks to Mark, Stephen and Mija for reading and appearing in these pages. Acknowledgements to the Varuna Writers' Centre (especially Deb Westbury), Yaddo and the Santa Fe Art Institute for providing space and time to write, funding for which was also provided by the Department of Culture and the Arts Western Australia. Gratitude to the faculty and students of the University of Houston Creative Writing Program and the members of the Out of the Asylum Writers Group, particularly Kevin Prufer, Beth Lyons, Ange Mlinko, Shane McCauley and Martha Serpas. Final thanks to Georgia and Wendy at Fremantle Press.

Poems have been previously published in *The Australian* ('To Robert Thompson'), *Australian Poetry* ('The Break', 'At the Ballarat Art Gallery'), *Australian Book Review* ('After a girl goes missing'), *Best Australian Poems 2012* ('To Robert Thompson'), *Best Australian Poems 2013* ('The break'), *Cordite* ('Directions', 'Eurydice speaks', 'Tacit knowledge'), *dirtcakes* ('Leonora 2010'), *Going Down Swinging* ('Back in Perth'), *Green Mountains Review* ('TV pastoral'), *Pamplemousse* ('Family rule'), *Stand Magazine* ('The fish'), *Sun-Herald Extra* ('Holiday'), *Westerly* ('Sundays', 'Donnelly River, 13', 'North of the river' and 'The path to the dam') and *Cullen Wines Poetry Collection* ('Terroir').

First published 2015 by
FREMANTLE PRESS
25 Quarry Street, Fremantle 6160
(PO Box 158, North Fremantle 6159)
Western Australia
www.fremantlepress.com.au

Cover design Ally Crimp
Cover photograph Orien Harvey, 'The Gap, Albany, WA'
Printed by Lightning Source, Victoria, Australia

National Library of Australia
Cataloguing-in-Publication entry

Maling, Caitlin, author, 1985–
Conversations I've never had / Caitlin Maling
ISBN: 9781925162028 (paperback)
Australian poetry.
Western Australia—poetry.

A823.4

Government of **Western Australia**
Department of **Culture and the Arts**

lotterywest
supported

Fremantle Press is supported by the State Government through the
Department of Culture and the Arts.

Australian Government

Australia Council
for the Arts

Publication of this title was assisted by the Commonwealth Government
through the Australia Council, its arts funding and advisory body.

www.ingramcontent.com/pod-product-compliance
Lightning Source LLC
Chambersburg PA
CBHW021156090426
42740CB00008B/1109